Library of Congress Cataloging in Publication Data
Gantz, David.   The Genie Bear with the light brown hair word book.
Summary: Genie Bear introduces his friends to words beginning with each letter of the alphabet.
1. English language—Alphabet—Juvenile literature. 2. Vocabulary—Juvenile literature. [1. Vocabulary] I. Title.
PE1155.G3   428.1   AACR2
Library of Congress Catalog Card Number 81-43000   ISBN: 0-385-17528-0

The Genie Bear With The Light Brown Hair

Word Book

by David Gantz

Doubleday & Company, Inc., Garden City, New York

"I love ketchup!" said Moxy Mouse. Moxy loved ketchup so much that he put it on everything he ate.

He put ketchup on roast beef, tuna fish, vegetable salad . . . he even put it on ice cream and lollypops.

One morning, while trying to put some ketchup on his scrambled eggs, Moxy came upon a very stubborn bottle. The ketchup just would not come out. Moxy shook the bottle until he was exhausted. Still no ketchup.

Thank goodness you stopped shaking me!

For setting me free, Moxy Mouse, I grant you three wishes.

Moxy had never heard a talking bottle and before he could shake it again, out popped Genie Bear with the light brown hair.

Aladdin didn't drive such a hard bargain.

Make it twenty-seven and it's a deal.

Cc

And for wish number three, Captain Swifty and a tale about "C".

Colossal!

A story about the sea, Captain?

No, Moxy, it's about "C"...

...as in Candy.

Calico Cat took his cousin, a child called Carl, to the carnival. Now, Carl craved candy—couldn't get his fill. So, the cousins collected all the candy and confection that they could carry and Carl carelessly consumed it all.

Carousel

Chocolate ice cream...

Custard.

ICE CREAM

First, there was cotton candy.

Classy!

Then he had a container of Cheerful Charley's candy corn.

Cheerful Charley's Candy Corn

Carl had some cakes, cookies, and chocolate-covered cherries.

Then he had some Cracker Jack, candy canes, chocolate chips, coconut creams, Chuckles . . .

and clustered peanuts, cinnamon hots, cherry drops, candied apples, Chunkys, ice cream, colas, cashews, cupcakes, and caramels.

Jack and Jill jogged up the hill
To fetch a jar of jam.
The other side was made of jellies
They slipped and slid down
on their bellies.

Yahoo!
Yodel-o-lay-Yee-o.
A yodeler yodeling
Yonder is a yodeler.
Are you Yellowbirds?
Yup.
Yep.
A yellow warbler in a yolk
A yak in a yoke
YALE
Y-E-S.
Why?
YIELD
A young Yorkie yapping at some yellow yarn
Yap Yap Yap
A yogi practicing Yoga
"Y" indeed.

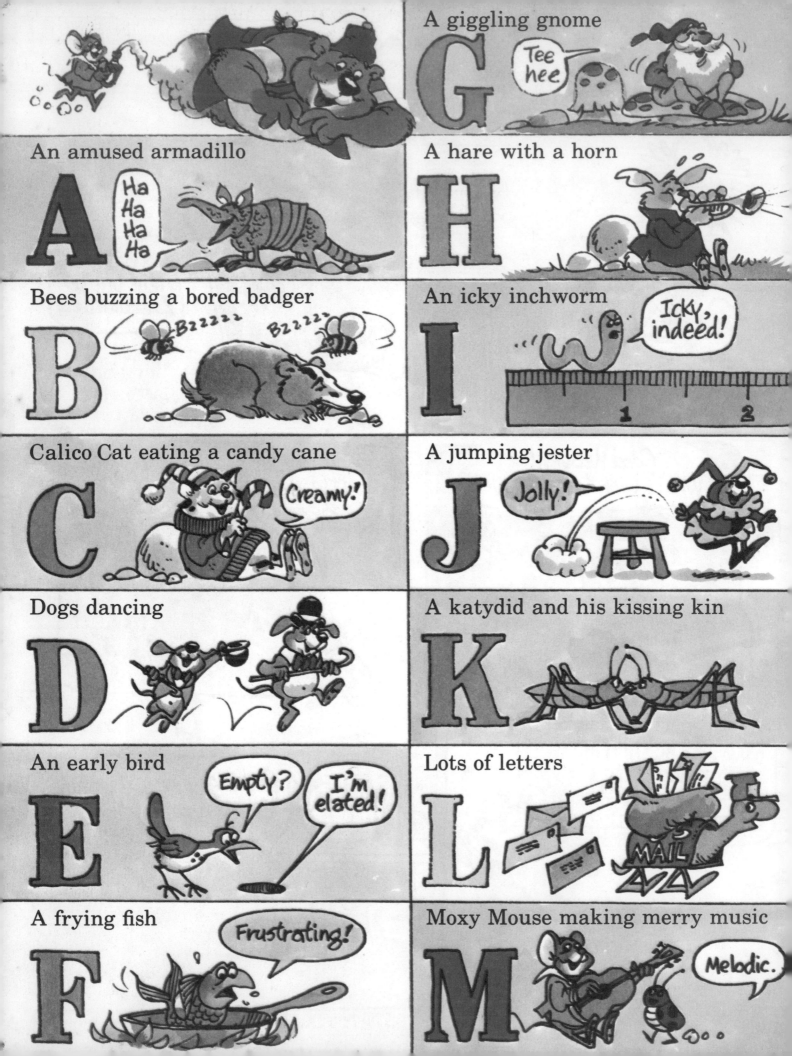